Praise for

MAKE YOUR IDEA MATTER

"A little book with a very big message. Your idea is worth a great story, well told."
—SETH GODIN

"Every story you tell is a choice, and the choices you make matter. For best results, make the choice to read this book."
—CHRIS GUILLEBEAU, AUTHOR OF *THE $100 STARTUP*

"*Make Your Idea Matter* is a book that's easy to get into and hard to escape. Full of valuable, original, engaging content.

Bernadette Jiwa has been likened to 'a female Seth Godin' and I have to agree."
—ROBERT GERRISH, DIRECTOR OF FLYING SOLO, AUSTRALIA'S MICRO BUSINESS COMMUNITY

"The most brilliant people I have known have the rare ability to distill complexity to an essence. This is what Bernadette Jiwa does for entrepreneurs in *Make Your Idea Matter*!"
—MARK SCHAEFER, AUTHOR OF *RETURN ON INFLUENCE* AND *THE TAO OF TWITTER*

"If I discover one useful insight in a business book, I consider the time well spent. This surprising little book delivers them in spades!"
—TOM ASACKER, AUTHOR OF *A CLEAR EYE FOR BRANDING*

"Now is your time to make a difference, your time to be the best at what you love doing, your time to use your skills to enrich not only your own life, but the lives of each and every individual you do business with.

More and more small businesses are taking impressive leads in their industries, making giant multinationals look cumbersome and unfriendly in comparison. You can do the same, and the first thing on your "to do" list should be to read this book.

Bernadette has written a fantastic collection of stories to inspire, to provoke, to make you think, to generate ideas, and to bring your business to the next level."
—DAVID AIREY, AUTHOR OF *LOGO DESIGN LOVE*

MAKE YOUR IDEA MATTER

MAKE
YOUR
IDEA
MATTER

STAND OUT WITH A BETTER STORY

BERNADETTE JIWA

The Story of Telling Press
Australia

Published in Australia by The Story of Telling Press.

www.thestoryoftelling.com

Portions of this book have appeared previously on
TheStoryofTelling.com blog.

Library of Congress Cataloging-in-Publication Data

Jiwa, Bernadette
Make your idea matter : stand out with a better story / by Bernadette Jiwa
p. cm.
1. Marketing. 2. Business Development. I. Title.
II. Title: Make your idea matter.

ISBN 978-1478394846

Printed in the United States of America

Book and Jacket Design: Reese Spykerman
Jacket Image: Veer

10 9 8 7 6 5 4 3 2 1

First Edition

For Mam and Dad

CONTENTS

MAKE YOUR IDEA MATTER

MAKE YOUR IDEA MATTER

INTRODUCTION

The path to success is littered with great ideas poorly marketed. Don't let yours be one of them.

Make Your Idea Matter is a call to action for entrepreneurs, emerging brands and anyone with a great idea, who knows that to stand out in today's noisy world they need to tell a better story.

It is full of bite-sized business and brand storytelling ideas originally sparked on Bernadette Jiwa's award-winning business blog TheStoryofTelling.com. Use this book as both inspiration and guide to help you tell the best stories you can tell about your business, your ideas and the work that matters to you.

You don't have to start on page one and work your way through, or even read it from front to back. Each topic stands on its own so dip in and out. Reawaken a thought or an idea you've already had. Spark new ones. Discover different ways of thinking about what you do and how you tell your story. Then go make *your* idea matter.

A LOVE NOTE TO ENTREPRENEURS

If you're doing your best work.

If you touched one person.

If it makes a difference to a handful.

If you're building a legacy, not just an empire.

If your values are front and centre.

If you're launching ideas from the heart.

If you understand why you're doing this.

If it doesn't have to matter to everyone.

If you care.

If you can see the world as it isn't.

If passion is your master.

If possibility feeds your soul.

If meaning is your currency.

If you embrace failure alongside success.

If permission doesn't get in your way.

If understanding the problem to be solved matters.

If people are your inspiration.

If you could change one thing.

If you know the questions to ask and aren't afraid of the answers.

If you could ask for anything today, would 'this' be it?

If not this, then what?

THEY MISS US NOW WE'RE GONE

The shopping malls are empty and the big department store owners are worried. They've finally got the memo. They realise that they can't out-stock Amazon, or price match the guy from Seoul selling wallets on eBay. So they're trying to woo us back with loyalty cards, air miles and faster ways to checkout our less-than-five items.

They miss us now we've gone, to buy a hand-crafted necklace online from designer and metalsmith Megan Auman, or a one-of-a-kind lamp, which Philippa Stanton makes using vintage maps.

We've moved on without them, while they kept buying double-page spreads in the local newspaper.

The world has changed. You don't have to compete with the big guys. They are the ones at a disadvantage now. You have everything you need to bring your ideas to life. To do work you care about, and to tell the story about what you do to people who want to listen.

It might be too late for the big guys to matter, but it's not too late for you.

YOU'VE GOT A BUSINESS IDEA; NOW WHAT?

I'm sure you've heard the story about how Richard Branson chartered a private plane when his flight to Puerto Rico was cancelled, and how he used a chalk board to pitch the idea of sharing that plane with fellow passengers. Although he wasn't planning to turn this event into a long-term business venture at the time, Richard still had to create a value proposition in order to get people interested that day.

He had to begin by asking himself these questions, progressing to number five when he decided to launch Virgin Atlantic Airways.

1. Do people want what I'm planning to make or offer?

2. How can I create and deliver it at a price they are willing to pay?

3. Can this product or service deliver on the promises I make to people?

4. How will I let people know about what I've created?

5. Can I generate enough money to build on my idea?

The answers to these five simple questions form the foundation of every business in existence.

Have you answered them yet?

WHAT MAKES AN IDEA MATTER?

Ideas are formed in the mind but triumph in the heart.

Your fabulous, worthy, well-thought-out ideas might have logical foundations, but logic is not what will convince people to rally to your cause or click the "Buy Now" button.

So begin everything from where your audience is. Set out to deliver to them the feelings they want to feel. Your idea must matter to them, not just to you.

WHAT IS A BRAND?

The American Marketing Association defines a brand as, "a name, term, design, symbol, or any other feature that identifies one seller's good or service as distinct from those of other sellers."

That definition might be a good starting point, but brands are much more to us than designs and symbols that differentiate. There is an infinite number of definitions of a brand. Here are just twenty:

A brand is…

1.   A promise.

2.   The way we differentiate this from that.

3.   Whatever the customer believes about a company.

4.   A feeling created.

5.   The tangible representation of personal or company values.

6.   A set of expectations met.

7.   The way a person or company communicates what they do and why they do it.

8.   Trust built between a customer and a business.

9.   A company asset.

10.   Your word.

11.   A set of unique benefits.

12.   Reasons to buy, or buy into, something.

13.   A story we tell ourselves.

14.   Communication with and without words.

15.   A symbol of belonging.

16.   Signals sent.

17.   A waymarker.

18.   The experience a customer has.

19.   A complete field guide to a business.

20.   The impression that's left at the last interaction.

What's your definition?

WHEN THE FACTS ARE NO LONGER ENOUGH

The window on analysis is shrinking. People are moving so fast now that they don't have time to think. They're scanning, swiping, clicking, liking, tweeting and moving on at full velocity. They're making decisions based on feelings, not facts. They are often choosing not because of what they think, but because of how something makes them feel.

What does this mean for your business?

If you want people to act, you must make them feel.

If they say 'I'll think about it', you've lost them; they're gone and on to the next thing.

WELL-DESIGNED MOMENTS BUILD BRANDS

When the airline tells you that lost luggage is just a fact of life, or the sales assistant can't exchange a faulty shirt on the spot because of company policy, that moment is a crack in the foundation of the brand. In that moment, you begin to disconnect and feel like you don't belong.

Every brand is built on the feelings and experiences it delivers to customers in the blink of an eye.

Returns should be made as easy as purchases. Cancelling subscriptions should be as easy as signing up. It rarely is.

The trick is to see the moment when the bubble bursts as an opportunity to deepen the relationship. Instead of shrugging off a mistake or letting customers fend for themselves, why not offer empathy? The opportunity to turn a '404' error-message Web page into a well-designed moment is open to everyone.

ONE THING YOU CAN LEARN FROM THE WORLD'S GREATEST MARKETER

Yesterday I Googled Seth Godin. This is not something I normally do—not because I never read his blog, but because I already have it bookmarked on my browser's toolbar. The search results made me chuckle. You see, Seth has been circled by over 95,000 people on Google+ and he has never posted a single update there. He has a very smart profile page, but that's it.

Seth's strategy is simple and effective. His focus is on building one asset, his own blog, where he posts great content every day, and all roads lead back to Seth's blog.

Here's the takeaway for every single business and brand:

Keep the home fires burning. Wherever the foundation of your business is, focus there. If you've got a tiny bookstore or a chain of juice bars, make them the kind of place that people seek out and want to come back to. If your business has a virtual home online, make it *the* place where people come to be inspired, motivated and educated.

As the guys at 37signals would say, make it the place where you generously "out-teach the competition."

Keep your home fires burning. Make your business or platform the place where people want to gather. Then make your ideas matter.

REFRAMING HOW YOU THINK ABOUT CUSTOMERS

How many business books have you read that urged you to think about how to capture the attention of your 'prospects'? Quite a few, I reckon; I've read them, too, and something about the use of that word in particular always makes me squirm. A 'prospect' by definition is either a potential source of profit or a likely customer. Nothing wrong with that, you might say. We're all in business to make a profit—no profit, no business. True. But viewing your potential customers as walking wallets is another thing entirely.

If you're thinking about the people who you hope will buy from you simply as 'prospects', customers, clients, consumers, patrons, corporations or entities, you're not only missing the point of doing business; you're also blinkering yourself to a huge opportunity.

The products and services you want to sell will not succeed in the market if you don't address the emotional wants of 'real people'. It's not enough just to fulfil the material needs of 'prospects'.

A business (your business) needs to look past the labels it gives the people it serves, and see their hopes, dreams, fears and aspirations.

Seeing beyond the 'prospect' label enabled Pebble Technology to tell people the story of how their product—a customisable 'smart watch' that uses Internet-connected apps—will fit into their lives.

Now cyclists and runners can get speed and distance data; and golfers will soon be able to see their exact distance from the green. Pebble Technology raised over $10 million in a few weeks on Kickstarter, not because 'prospects' needed a Pebble, but because 'real people' wanted one.

Customers can get a hundred good-enough watches on Amazon. Real people become fans of things that they care about.

CREATE WHAT PEOPLE CAN'T LIVE WITHOUT—EIGHT QUESTIONS TO ASK BEFORE LAUNCHING A BUSINESS IDEA

Where would you be without your laptop, your smart phone, Google, take-away coffee cups and quick-drying nail polish? While you're busy navigating your day today, think about what you couldn't live without, the stuff that makes your life that little bit easier. All those things you didn't even realise you needed, until someone brought them to market.

Every product or service ever created was born from a problem that needed to be solved, or a desire that was waiting to be fulfilled.

Understanding the problem to be solved is the reason we have online check-in, fruit smoothies in bottles, and the Genius Bar.

So how do you begin to understand the problem that's waiting to be solved?

You stand in your customer's shoes, see her world as it is, and then create a better version of it.

That's how a Sydney mum invented GameTag (a clever loss-prevention device for Nintendo DS games) and why Facebook became part of the fabric of our lives.

Here are eight questions to ask yourself before you launch an idea:

1. Why am I creating this product or service, and why now?

2. Who exactly is the product or service for?

3. What's the competition?

4. Do I need to worry about the competition?

5. How is this different and better?

6. How do I research, test, launch, market, distribute, sell, build and scale my business idea?

7. Do I need to research, test, and scale, or should I just press Go?

8. How will I know when I've succeeded?

WHAT'S THE PURPOSE OF A BRAND STORY?

If you've got a great product or a killer service, why do you need a brand story? You only have to look as far as your local café or boutique fashion labels to see that not all brands are created equal, and what usually separates the successes from the failures is a good story.

The story makes the product better.

The Versalette story from {r}evolution apparel actually makes the product better in the eyes of the consumer. When she buys a Versalette—an environmentally friendly garment that can be worn in 15 ways—she can tell herself a story about what she believes is important. She can send a signal to the world about her conscious-consumption values, and she gets to be a trendsetter into the bargain.

Any business or brand can add a meaningless 'me too' tagline under their logo, but if it's just pixels filling up white space, what's the point? If your story (not just the words you write, but your staff, values, customer experience and so on) doesn't make what you do better, then you're missing a huge opportunity to help people care enough to invest in you.

WHY YOU NEED TO THINK DIFFERENTLY ABOUT SUCCESS

From the outside looking in, success looks so easy. Successful people make it all look a bit like falling off a log. It's easy to think that success happens in the moment, or is catalysed by one major event, like being stranded while travelling, deciding to charter a plane and then selling tickets to other passengers by scrawling the details on a blackboard, as Richard Branson did. Eureka!

In reality, success doesn't happen like this. The opportunities you've created didn't just fall into your lap. They are not the result of one giant leap, but are the product of a million tiny decisions you've been making every day for years.

It's the small choices, not the momentous one-off decisions, that define us.

Danielle LaPorte didn't begin building her multi-layered business on the day she launched her website. She was laying those foundations long before she ever came up with the Fire Starter Sessions, her inspirational digital program for aspiring entrepreneurs. And although the beginning of Virgin Atlantic provides a great story, Richard Branson was exercising his entrepreneurial muscle long before he chartered that flight.

Success, like the exercise that gives you washboard abs, is a habit. It's the daily practice of making small choices that add up in the end. It's about doing what you said you'd do, even though nobody but you will notice, and about knowing in your gut why that matters.

HOW TO MAKE
YOUR MESSAGE STICK

I read an interesting fact on the last few pages of my friend Mark's new book, *Return on Influence*. Apparently, most people abandon a business book after reading one-third of it. This is an audience who decided they believed in the idea, the author or maybe the title and cover design enough to invest, only to abandon the book just as they were getting started. We have so many choices now, that we even choose to abandon the things that we choose.

How do you hold people's attention and get your message to stick?

Think about any book you've read; what you remember are the stories. I remember how Klout's founder Joe Fernandez found himself housebound with time on his hands after he'd had his jaws wired, and that this was when he began exploring social scoring and planning world domination. I remember Mark's story about seeing a friend's poor review of a restaurant he was at, and how that affected his experience that evening.

> *"People don't want more information.*
> *They are up to their eyeballs in information.*
> *They want faith.*
> *Faith in you, your goals, your success, in the story*
> *you tell."*
> —ANNETTE SIMMONS

Take a leaf from the book of one of the most successful non-fiction authors of our time, Malcolm Gladwell. From the very opening lines in the introduction of his international bestseller *Blink*, Gladwell hooks us with the intriguing story of Gianfranco Becchina, who offered an ancient artifact to The Getty Museum for $10 million, and we can't wait to read on.

Make your facts real by painting an unforgettable picture with a story.

A LESSON FROM THE MOST ICONIC ADVERT IN THE WORLD

The 1971 Coca-Cola 'Hilltop' advertisement is known as one of the best-loved and most influential ads in TV history. The advertisement featured a multi-cultural group of teenagers singing, "I'd like to teach the world to sing (in perfect harmony)", and it portrayed a positive message of hope and unity.

Harvey Gabor, a member of the original creative team for 'Hilltop', says that the lines in the advert talk about the world, but it really speaks to one person.

No matter what you're pitching, selling or talking about, talk to one person.

You might want to appeal to a hundred, or even a million, people. Do that by making your idea matter one person at a time.

Speak to that person.

TURN UP THE VOLUME ON YOUR MISSION

In the tiny town of Cardigan in Wales, jean artisans from the abandoned factory are making jeans again, thanks to David and Clare Hieatt, the founders of Hiut Denim. Their mission is not to make the most jeans, but to make the best jeans.

Whatever your idea, whatever you market, sell or promote, whether it's a cause, art, products or services, the way you differentiate yourself from your competitors is by turning up the volume on the story of your mission.

Products can be similar, but missions are unique.

You don't want people to buy your stuff; you want to matter to them. You want them to care about your brand. To believe in what you do. To 'buy in'. Part of your mission is to get those people, not everyone, but the ones you care about, to care.

The mission of an artist isn't to sell her stuff to the masses; it's to sell the ideas conveyed in those things, maybe to just 1000 true fans. The artist buys into the idea that she not only expresses herself through her art, but also helps others to do the same. Her mission is to shape culture, to communicate beauty, stimulate thought and make an emotional connection.

Hiut Denim's mission isn't to persuade the guy who buys $30 jeans every few months at Target that investing four times that amount in a pair of hand-crafted jeans is a good idea. Their mission is to change something, as well as make something, and to bring their customers and fans along for the ride.

The desire to change something and shape culture over time is part of any great brand mission. This principle applies to Etsy store owners, authors, Burton Snowboards and Dollar Shave Club alike.

Your product might be similar, but your mission is unique.

All you have to do is turn up the volume by amplifying your difference and telling a better story than the competition.

THE PURPOSE OF BRANDING

If a brand is more than just a logo, a tagline and the colour of the packaging, then what is branding?

Branding is not something that's arranged on the surface, like a stiffly coiffed hairstyle on a fashion model. It takes place from the inside out, so successful brands and ideas are founded on a great mission, a story that we want to believe in.

Everything you do to tell that story—from your brand name, to your social media interactions—must amplify what you stand for, and communicate to the world why people should care that you brought this thing to life in the first place.

Branding is shorthand, not a shortcut.

NINE ELEMENTS OF THE PERFECT PITCH

It doesn't matter how good your idea is if nobody knows. If you want to make your idea matter, then you'll need to get better at helping people to understand why it should.

Preparation

It's hard to sell anything without having a plan and putting some effort in beforehand. Even the guy who walks up to a girl in a bar has put on a clean shirt and rehearsed what he's going to say.

Emotion

A pitch is based less on logic and more on tapping into emotions. It's less about presenting information and more about persuading people deep down. Studies from the *Journal of Advertising Research* show that we are twice as likely to be persuaded by emotion than by facts. You must make people care before you can persuade them to believe.

Story and substance

Delivery is important but falls flat without a great story. The words you use and the stories you tell matter.

Passion
You're not simply asking people to buy your idea; you're per-suading them to 'buy into' it, and into you. This will not happen if you can't communicate your genuine passion to the audience.

A problem
Understand the problem you solve, and communicate that.

An answer
You've demonstrated that you know what the problem is; now reveal your valuable solution.

Simplicity
You've got nine seconds to convince people that you are the one. Don't overload them with information; concentrate on what really matters to them.

Confidence
You're asking people to bet on you, to embrace the fact that there is no certainty in most decisions they make. If you don't believe in yourself and your idea, how can you expect others to?

Practice
Delivery is part science, part theatre, and part art. It can be learned with practice.

WHY ARE YOU IN BUSINESS?

When you don't answer the phone after the third ring. When the wait staff you hired forget to look people in the eye. When you make it easy for people to sign up and say yes, but penalise them for changing their minds, you are forgetting the only reason your business exists and what its success depends on.

You are in business to acknowledge the significance of, and create meaning for, clients and customers. Your job is to practice the art of making people matter, by putting their wants and needs front and centre in everything you do.

The reason you're in business is to make peoples' lives better.

Every word you write, meal you serve or pixel you paint is nothing without an audience to consume it and, more important, care about it.

So here's the question you need to ask:

How does what you do, make, serve or sell make life better for your clients and customers? The same rules apply whether you're Richard Branson or a boutique design studio in Melbourne.

WHY YOU NEED A MISSION MORE THAN A WEBSITE

Nine times out of ten, when I consult with clients they are impatient to get to work on the tactical side of spreading their idea. They wonder about which website and social media platforms to use. They worry about design elements and website functionality. Maybe you do, too?

Of course you want to get your idea out there into the world. But while tactics are necessary to spread your idea, in the long run it's more important that you first have an idea that matters.

Many of the answers to the tactical stuff can be found with a 60-second search. But you can't Google your unique mission or vision; that's why it is the foundation of your business or cause. The same rules apply to global corporations, solitary artists or tiny bistros.

Tactics help to promote your idea, but a clear strategy is what really sells it. The first question you need to ask is 'why will people care about this?' and not 'how will we get them to buy this?'

Blake Mycoskie started a company that made comfy, lightweight shoes, but the story doesn't end there. For every pair of shoes bought from his online shoe store, TOMS, another pair is donated to children in a developing country who have none. TOMS Shoes pioneered the 'One for One' movement, and in the process they built a brand that people could care about buying from.

People don't buy into your platform; they buy into the difference you make.

WHY 'HOW TO' IS THE WRONG PLACE TO START

Focusing on the 'how to' stops you from thinking about the why and the what first.

Most companies wonder how they will get their product noticed, before thinking about why on earth it will matter to customers. In a world where we're bombarded with messages that we can choose to ignore, more of the same in a brighter package or more colourful box isn't what we're searching for. It isn't what we tell our friends about, either.

When customers and investors (or maybe even you) don't understand your story or how to communicate it, your ideas and your products blend in. Your brand fails to connect with your audience, and they don't have a reason to buy into what you do and why you do it.

When people really 'get it', your brand has the potential to attract investors, dominate a niche and reinvent a market.

Communicating the essence of a big vision is what has always powered, and will continue to power, successful brands.

Hiut Denim and TOMS Shoes started with a 'big why'. The 'how to' came later. The story of the 'big why' makes the product better. When your brand story makes an emotional connection with your customers, they're more likely to spread the word about who you are and what you do. Your customers have a bond with your brand. They buy in.

It doesn't matter whether you sell jeans, shoes, a writing workshop, design services or even deodorant.

Brand leaders and change makers always ask 'why this' before they work on 'how to'.

That's why we believe in them.

GIVING A DAMN
IS SERIOUSLY UNDERRATED

My boys had a sick rat. At the vet's, she was weighed and had her chest listened to. The vet sent her home with an antibiotic and instructions. If she didn't get better very quickly, the outlook wasn't good.

At ten the following morning, I got a call from the vet nurse. She asked how Luna was doing, if she was breathing any easier, or eating anything yet, and if we had been able to get the medicine into her. The nurse reminded me that it was okay to call back if we had any concerns. We were having this conversation about a $12 rat that had another year of life in her either way, and I just can't stop thinking (and talking) about it.

Nobody called the day after my son had a biopsy taken from his neck to see if he had a rare tumour (thankfully he didn't). Nobody called when they lost his school book order or when we were without Internet service for two weeks.

When nobody calls, we interpret that as 'nobody cares'. When they *do* call, it blows us away and we tell ten friends.

That's your opportunity.

YOUR BRAND IS A STORY

I'll never forget the day my son read his first word. We were living in the UK at the time. I was driving through town that day when he piped up from the back, "that's ASDA". I whipped my head around and saw him pointing an impossibly tiny finger at the huge ASDA sign towering above the road. He was just 18 months old. He'd barely learned to speak at all and yet he was forming an impression of a brand. Making meaning from a set of experiences he'd had and then tying them together.

Your brand is a story. A window on awareness. More than just a logo or a price ticket. That story is shaped by the experiences people have around everything you do, from typeface to copy and even how they felt and what they saw on their very first shopping trips with their mum. It has the power to become the stuff of myth and legend (even for a tiny audience) if you enable people to see themselves as part of the story, too.

WHEN WHAT YOU'RE SELLING ISN'T WHAT YOU'RE SELLING

Yesterday I skipped the early gym session, packed up my Mac-Book and headed out to the hair salon. This particular salon runs a no-appointment-system; it's first-come, first-served. So I got there almost an hour before they opened, sat on the ground outside and worked. Ten minutes later, another lady arrived; twenty minutes after her, yet another, who I'd seen before. With fifteen minutes to opening time, a grandmother showed up, excitedly chatting to two little girls about how they'd be talking to Carmel and she'd know what was best for them to do.

By 9:00 a.m., there were six of us all queuing for the same stylist. By 9:05, there was a three-hour wait for a $20 trim with Carmel, even though there were at least four other stylists available right away. A couple of people chose to wait, and some were reluctantly bumped to other stylists.

I watched Carmel work all morning. The first question she asked, before she even picked up a pair of scissors, was, "Is this for the graduation, and if not, when is that?" The next client was asked how long before her three-month trip overseas; it was apparently important not to put too much colour in this time round, so that the timing would be just right for the last colouring before her trip. Carmel explained to the elderly lady who couldn't cope with a two-hour wait that she had a couple of colour clients already, but she'd tell the other stylist what to do. I heard her reminding her colleague about the frailty of the hair and how she needed to use the mildest possible products. The granddaughters were having back-to-school trims. They were done in five minutes by another stylist, while the grandmother came to have a chat with Carmel as she mixed bleach.

Of course there are others in this salon who can cut and colour almost as well as Carmel can, but that's not what people who are willing to wait for an hour or two, maybe more, are buying. She's not selling a $20 haircut; she's selling something people crave even more than looking just right for their son's graduation: caring, connection, belonging and yes, even love. All of which take something ordinary and make it extraordinary.

Your business needs people who care this much. Often your products and services don't need more bells and whistles. They just need a little more love.

ONLY WE...

Starbucks has been the only coffee chain since the '90s that can sell a Frappuccino®. Try selling a whipped iced coffee with that name somewhere else and you'll be busted by the intellectual property police. You can't call your customer service centre the Genius Bar® either—that service mark belongs to Apple—but that doesn't mean you can't have one.

Even a few short years ago, the opportunities to confidently say 'only we' abounded. Features and benefits, along with factories and platforms, were difficult to duplicate. Today we have one-man magazine publishing houses—such as the micropublishing house Mountain & Pacific, run by Thom Chambers—and we have very different opportunities to tell the 'only we' story to our clients and customers.

This might sound like bad news, but actually it's the best news for tiny app developers, boutique designers and solo entrepreneurs. The 'only we' of the industrial era has become the 'only I' and 'only with us' of the digitally connected era. Anyone with a great idea, who tells a better story, can rally a tribe on the crowd-funding platform Kickstarter. Co-working spaces, laptops, Wi-Fi connections and social media platforms have all made the world smaller and the opportunities, greater.

Now is your time. Now was always a good time to start.

IT'S ALL BEEN DONE BEFORE

This is what I call 'the pioneer's lament'.

It goes something like this:

You have a great idea. It could be for a product, a service, a book, a blog post, or a new kind of dog food. You start planning, taking notes, visualising the impact of said thing on the world; then the research kicks in and you discover it's been done before.

Bubble popped.

The bad news is, it's *all* been done before. The good news is, it doesn't matter, because it hasn't been done by *you*.

According to Amazon.com, 7,012 books (and counting) have been written about 'startups'. That didn't stop Eric Ries from having a *New York Times* bestseller with *The Lean Startup,* or stop Portfolio.com from dubbing 2011 as 'the year of the lean startup'.

The quota for ideas hasn't been used up just yet. The capacity for experiencing difference hasn't been reached.

What makes anything you do unique is *your* voice. The story that only you can tell, from a perspective that nobody else can have. There is more than one way to say something important that needs to be said, and there are a million ways to bring ideas that matter to the world.

TWENTY WAYS TO NURTURE YOUR IDEAS

1. Create an idea-saving system.
Find tools that work for you. Moleskine notebooks or the Evernote app, anyone?

2. Be ready to capture ideas anywhere.
J.K. Rowling tells the story of how Harry Potter "fell into her head" on a train journey.

3. Step away from the computer.
Pick up a pen, doodle, make a mindmap, take photos. Use both sides of your brain.

4. Understand your creative process.
Be aware of what drives you. Reflect on how you make things happen.

5. Use tools that inspire you.
Leather journals, coloured pens, scrapbooks, green ink….

6. Be on a mission.
Why does the idea excite you? Why this idea, why now? What difference will it make in the world?

7. Begin with the end in mind.
Visualise the end product, the colour of the book cover, the texture of the paper, the graphics on the packaging.

8. Stand in the shoes of the people you want to affect.
Now create the thing that makes the biggest difference to them.

9. Set goals.
Have milestones you can reach. A launch date. Write them down, then stick to them.

10. Don't set goals.
Just go.

11. Follow hunches.
Trust your gut. Act on your wildest dreams.

12. Find quiet space.
Meditation, walks, getting closer to nature, time to journal. What works for you?

13. Plan meticulously.
Map out desired outcomes, skill sets, milestones, resources.

14. Work quickly.
Start to finish in a day.

15. Practice blue-sky thinking.
Ask "what if?"

16. Outsource.
Play to your strengths. Learn the skills you need to execute, and get help when you need it.

17. Try and fail.
Today's mistakes are the foundation for tomorrow's successes.

18. Focus.
Limit distractions. Shut yourself away. Use time management tools like the Pomodoro technique.

19. Do the work.
Hit Publish, press Send, hang the picture or launch the website. An idea without execution is just an idea; it has no impact on the world.

20. Do what it feels good to do.
Ideas that get you up early and keep you up late are the ones that matter.

THE SECRET TO CREATING PRODUCTS PEOPLE BUY

The secret to the success of Facebook, Pampers, Innocent drinks, Instagram, Basecamp and on and on, comes down to one thing: the ability to stand in the customer's shoes and see the world from that person's point of view.

Have you questioned what your client's worldview is lately?

What's important to your customers right now?

What are they excited about?

What are they struggling with?

What would they kill to know?

What stops them from achieving their dreams?

What do they crave or covet?

Why do they need you?

What will they gladly pay for?

How can you be part of their journey today?

What might they need tomorrow?

Your business is built on the foundations of a story that your customers want to believe in. Great products and services are created by understanding why they will care about that story.

EVEN THE BIG GUYS ARE GUESSING

The confectionary giant Cadbury experimented by launching a product on Google+. The launch was their best guess, and they went with it. Even they don't know for sure what will work and what won't. Yes, they pay people to help them with the process of being *more* sure, but they never really know until the idea is out there.

There are no guarantees, no way of knowing one hundred percent if you've got the right answer. Will that idea that's rattling around in your head work? There's only one way to know and that's to try it. Press Play, click Publish, set up your stall, take your first feedback—that's the opportunity. You have the chance to try and to fail or succeed, if not this time, then the next one, or the one after that.

How will you ever know unless you work hardest of all on getting it out there? Unless your idea is a revolutionary new pacemaker, there's room to make your very best guess and there's still time to change things tomorrow, after you launch.

THE STORY YOU TELL
IS A CHOICE

The story you tell is a choice.

Creating a series of lines in the sand.

Symbolic of values that you're not willing to compromise on.

Your brand can't be all things to everyone.

This and that.

The brands that stand out, that have soul, that win by being different, choose.

They choose to stand for something, and then make that something the foundation of their story.

What's your story? What lines in the sand have you chosen to draw?

THE APPLE STORE, BELONGING AND LOVE

What's the one thing you never find at an Apple Store? That thing you probably found in your hotel room when you checked in. The poorly expressed intention to customers that guarantees they will never come back. Oh, and it's most likely laminated and taped up in several places.

Ah yes… a list of rules.

I found that list pasted four times around our holiday getaway recently. Every poorly considered word told us what we *couldn't* do in the outdoor spa and what we *must* do. Every time we saw that note, we knew that we weren't trusted and didn't belong.

The Apple Store is a place without rules. No glass cases. No velvet ropes between the product and the customer. Everybody's welcome. That's part of the reason it's the busiest store in your city. Every single contact point invites you to experience the products. To explore, to touch, to play, to linger and belong. There are no barriers to intimacy. And that's exactly what your customers want from you. They want to know that they belong.

Before customers can allow your designs, copy, books and products to belong in their lives, they need to sense your intention.

They want to trust you and feel that you trust them, too.

Your clients want to be welcomed like a friend and wooed like a lover. They can feel your intention at every point of contact. It's your job to communicate that intention with all your heart and soul. Doesn't matter if you sell shoes, coffee, design, copy or connection. Making rules is lazy. Building trust and expressing intentions isn't easy, but it's worth it.

Have you found ways to create intimacy with your clients, either online or offline?

What businesses and brands do you love, and how do they create a feeling of belonging?

CHANGE HOW PEOPLE FEEL, NOT WHAT THEY DO

Every marketing decision you make should be prefaced with this question:

"How will it make her feel?"

Of course you want people to do something, but you need them to feel something first. When people feel, they act. The feeling is what leads to the doing.

Think about the websites and cafés you love to visit, the book titles that attract your attention and the things that you own or covet. Consider companies like TOMS shoes and their 'One for One' movement. They have found a way to tell a story that changes how you feel, not just how you think. It turns out that changing hearts, not just minds, is a great business strategy.

KNOWING FOR SURE

What you often want is a guarantee. The sure-fire thing. The one that cannot fail. You will ask, 'How will I know for sure?' and 'What's definitely going to stick?' You will question whether you are putting the cart before the horse, and then try to work out how 'most people in your shoes' put horses first to produce a winning product. That's the human reaction to uncertainty, and it's also what suffocates great ideas.

The best ideas are born from the uncertainty. Most people, in *any* shoes, build a winning product by getting over the fear. They just start. There are no guarantees. You need to be okay with that. Your certainty must come from knowing that you want to bring something great into the world. Take that knowing and use it as the catalyst for doing.

Without action in the midst of uncertainty, there would be no Instagram, Discovr apps or Liana Raine's Blueberry Basil Pops.

Once you start wondering about 'people in your shoes' and horses versus carts, the idea stops being important enough to matter.

Wonder just enough; then go do.

SOMETHING FOR EVERYONE

The artisan pop company Liana Raine doesn't make Pineapple Chilli ice-lollies for everyone. And plenty of people hated the picture book *Go The F**k To Sleep*, which became a bestseller by delighting parents with a particular worldview.

If everything were created for the market of everyone, there would be no room for art by Banksy, T-shirts by Threadless or $500 beats by Dr. Dre.

Your job is to tell the best story you can to the people who want to hear it. To surprise, delight and bring joy to those people and to gently close the door on the people who don't want to listen. Don't worry about converting the lifelong Egg McMuffin eater to your Green Juice detox regime. You don't have to make something for everyone.

Unsubscribers, critics and naysayers are a gift. Say a mental thanks to them for saving you the job of working out who your right people are. Then go out and do everything in your power to woo the people who matter.

HOW TO TELL
A GOOD BUSINESS STORY

"Start with the truth. Identify the worldview of the
people you need to reach. Describe the truth through
their worldview."
—Seth Godin

What picture are you painting of your business? Are you trying too hard to sound more professional, bigger, slicker, and more polished than the competition? Is your story riddled with jargon instead of illuminated by truth? Does it make customers feel something?

Jargon puts your clients to sleep, kills the conversa-
tion dead, and sucks the soul out of ideas.

Think of your business story as the first date. As a way to start establishing the kind of relationship that leaves people wanting more. Your story doesn't need to give all of the information; it simply needs to foster the next conversation. Here's some inspiration for you:

"Skype is software that enables the world's conversations. Millions
of individuals and businesses use Skype to make free video and voice
calls, send instant messages and share files with other Skype users.
Every day, people also use Skype to make low-cost calls to landlines
and mobiles."

At this point we don't know how the software works or what the system requirements are, and we don't need to. What we know so far hooks us and makes us want to know more.

From 37signals:
"Goodbye to bloat. Simple, focused software that does just what you need and nothing you don't."

So far we don't even know what kind of software this company creates (spreadsheets? databases?); we just expect it to be lean and easy to use. And so we take a second look.

From Hiut Denim:
"Do one thing well. We make jeans. That's it. Nothing else. No distractions. Nothing to steal our focus. No kidding ourselves that we can be good at everything. No trying to conquer the whole world. We just do our best to conquer our bit of it. So each day we come in and make the best jeans we know how. Use the best quality denims. Cut them with an expert eye. And then let our 'Grand Masters' behind the sewing machines do the rest."

Wow! I want to buy something from someone who is *that* passionate about what they do.

Is your story part of your product, and does your story make the product better?

THE ONE THING TO REMEMBER ABOUT WEBSITE TRAFFIC

Of course you want more traffic to your website. After all,

MORE EYEBALLS = MORE AWARENESS

MORE AWARENESS = MORE AUTHORITY

MORE AUTHORITY = MORE SUCCESS

MORE SUCCESS = MORE CHOICES

Behind that 'traffic', behind every statistic, every blip on your analytics, every search term that brought people to your site, behind every Tweet, Like and +1, is a person just like you, who wants to matter.

Think about that for a second. They, too, scraped ice off the windscreen this morning, took their kids to soccer practice last night and commuted to work so they could pay next week's grocery bill or next semester's college fees. And they found *you* by sitting on the other side of this screen, searching for something beyond information.

Remember them every time you sit down to post, design a product, or open your shop doors, and you'll do your best work, the kind of work that earns more than just traffic and eyeballs and authority.

BUILDING A CURRENCY OF TRUST

It's tempting, when selling your product, service or idea, just to focus on what it takes to make a particular transaction happen. That transaction might make a dent in the balance sheet in the short term, but it's important not to lose sight of what will make a long-term difference to your business and to focus on the legacy of the interaction.

The purpose of every interaction is not to sell your idea or your answer; it's to foster the next interaction and build trust.

Now more than ever, as our networks expand and we operate in the global village, far beyond our neighbourhoods, legacies are built on tiny transactions and leaps of faith.

Trust is built over time. Bit by bit. Interaction by interaction. Doesn't matter whether that's in your café, in your studio, or on your Facebook page.

BRANDS ARE SHAPED BY THE STORIES WE TELL OURSELVES

Coffee chic is not merely a creation of Starbucks, no more than flawless design is the singular domain of Apple. What these companies do with a clever brand story is make it easier for us to buy into the wants that we associate with being part of our story.

What we actually believe to be the truth about the brands we love has as much to do with trendy interactive spaces we enjoy lingering in and exploring, as it has to do with products we consume or want to talk about.

Brands are what customers perceive them to be and are never just about what marketing departments communicate about the products being bought and sold.

Back in the '70s, you could tell a story about who you were, depending on which brand of doll you played with (Barbie or Sindy), and what kind of bicycle you owned (who didn't want to own a 'Chopper' back then?). Those stories you told yourself mattered almost more than the things themselves, just as the stories your clients can tell themselves about doing business with you today matter.

Brands like Anthropologie and Lululemon shape aspirations and create a feeling of belonging. They are more than just places to shop.

What story can your customers tell themselves when they visit your website, use your product or walk into your store? Is it the one you hoped they would be telling?

WHY KNOWING WHAT TO LEAVE OUT MATTERS

The secret of any great book, movie, business, product, or service is in the editing.

As an entrepreneur or a creative person, your understanding of what to leave out is just as important as what you decide to leave in.

Christopher Nolan no doubt left hours and hours of carefully crafted shots and scenes from *Memento* in the cutting room, and the movie we saw was so much the better because of that. It doesn't matter whether you're designing an app or a shoe, framing a photo or a company, creating a course or a website, your editing decisions are the key to pulling the whole thing together. Like the perfect final cut, your product and brand story needs just the right combination of carefully selected elements.

Taking a metaphorical blue pencil to your 'baby' isn't easy. Sometimes you're too close to the work to understand which details really matter. And sometimes it's just too hard to toss hours of creative energy aside.

Take a step back and pretend you're not you; stand in your audience's shoes. And above all, don't wait for the day when the whole thing is perfect to bring it to the world. Even Christopher Nolan has made mistakes and continuity errors (54 were spotted in *Memento*), and lived to create another day.

WHAT SHOULD YOUR WEBSITE DO?

What you want your website to do is probably very different from what your customers want it to do. The trick (as with most elements of your business) is to build for customers and community first so you can realise the benefits later.

You want your website to:

1. Be on the first page in Google.

2. Attract customers.

3. Boost credibility.

4. Convert browsers into subscribers.

5. Change followers into fans.

6. Connect you to the right audience.

7. Make you money.

8. Increase your business, bottom line or popularity.

9. Make you look bigger, better, stronger, faster.

10. Tell a story that people want to believe.

Your customers want your website to:

1. Be exactly what they were looking for.

2. Give them a solution to a problem.

3. Tell them the answer.

4. Help them to understand.

5. Entertain or educate.

6. Connect them to people, ideas and things they care about.

7. Save them time.

8. Save them money.

9. Be clear and show them the way.

10. Focus on their wants and needs.

How is your business catering to your clients' wants, while fulfilling your needs?

HOW DO YOU DIFFERENTIATE YOUR IDEA?

Often the real value of the work you do isn't what's inside the package or in the ebook. In order to differentiate, you need to really understand the effect of what you do, sell, offer or deliver to people. I hope you'll consider asking yourself some of the questions on this list and maybe add a few of your own.

1. Why do you do what you do?

2. Does your story really define what you do?

3. What makes you and your product, service or business stand out?

4. What makes it blend in?

5. How is your product different?

6. How is your service special?

7. Are you delivering on your promise of being original, unique, the fastest, flexible, enduring, the best?

8. Can you create a new market and do something that hasn't been done before?

9. Can you reinvent something that's already been done and do it better?

10. How are you least like the competition?

11. What's not selling today that might sell if you marketed it in new ways tomorrow?

12. Could you produce something enduring, that's scalable?

13. Is it possible to create scarcity?

14. How is your product compelling?

15. Is your name evocative?

16. Does your work start conversations?

17. If not, how could you make that happen?

18. Are you giving people a sense of your purpose and values?

19. How does your product or service make people feel? Have you asked them?

20. What's your legacy?

BRAND NAMES ARE THE START OF THE STORY

From the moment the blue line appears on the pregnancy test and for the next 35 weeks, the one thing that obsesses most couples day and night while waiting for their new arrival is what they will call her. They compulsively leaf through baby-name books, trawl websites and test out sound combinations and meanings. They poll friends, and they write list upon list, crossing off here, adding there, agonising about the legacy of this one decision. Since time began, humans have instinctively understood that a name is the start of a story.

When we name our children, we are writing the opening lines of their first chapter. We want to give them names they can grow into. Their names are part of our vision of what we hope they will one day be in the world, and researchers have proven that names can have a lasting impact on outcomes for individuals in later life. Researcher David Figlio of Northwestern University in Illinois found that boys with names traditionally given to girls are more likely to misbehave than their counterparts with masculine names. Once these kids hit sixth grade, all of a sudden the rates of disciplinary problems skyrocket.

Names are not designed simply to identify; they really can take us in one direction or another. And so it goes with brand names, book titles and product names. Companies know that names can make or break them, that names build mystery, that they can form the basis of a movement or create cult status. That's why *Purple Cow* is a more compelling title than *Marketing for Today*, and why the name 'Innocent' was a genius way to begin the story of a juice company.

A great name can take you places that a good name can't. A truly great brand name makes room for a new story in people's hearts and minds and can position a good product beyond its utility.

Don't set out to name a company or product; set out to name the vision of what you want to see in the world. Design your brand name to create lofty expectations, to make people believe something, not just notice it, and to signal your difference to the world.

THE ART OF GIVING PEOPLE WHAT THEY REALLY WANT

The group fitness instructor at our local gym is exceptionally good at giving people what they really want. During a tough early morning Body Pump® session, he doesn't talk about resting heart rate or thermogenesis. Duane punctuates those last thirty seconds of effort by telling us that this is how we'll get Michelle Obama arms. So we just keep on lifting.

Gym goers want beauty as much as health. Wearers of five-inch heels want longer legs more than they want remarkable shoes.

Understanding what your customers and clients desire is the key to giving them what they really want. That might not be what they think they showed up for in the first place.

BE COMPELLING

The path to success is not determined simply by the ability to have great ideas. What makes a product, service, cause or idea fly is the ability to understand its relevance to real people and to sell that.

The MP3 player is one of the best examples of a product for which being first didn't matter one jot. Lots of people came selling their tech and specs before Apple launched the iPod, but they just didn't tell a compelling story. People can't fall in love with 32MB and user interfaces.

But "1000 songs in your pocket"—now that's compelling!

The path to success is littered with great ideas poorly marketed.

Compelling is empowering people to take action.

"You've got to get on the phone and take the money out of your pocket. Don't go to the pub tonight. PLEASE! Stay in and give us the money. There are people dying NOW!
So give me the money."
— BOB GELDOF ON LIVE AID

Compelling is telling people (as IKEA'S tagline urged them) to "Love where you live", rather than asking them to buy your flat-pack furniture and a red cushion they probably don't need.

And compelling is you amplifying your passion enough to tell people why you're different. Just like the Dollar Shave Club did when it launched its economical, high-quality razor subscription and delivery service. Then you show customers what that difference could mean to them.

ADVERTISING IS NOT REAL MARKETING

Think about the people you do business with and the brands you care about. Are you drawn in by their advertising or by their marketing story?

That full-colour advert in the Sunday supplement is a tactic. So is the expensive, shiny new website you're having built and those letterpress business cards you spent a fortune on. Tactics help you to communicate your message. Real marketing makes it stick.

Real marketing is built into what you do and why you do it. It's part of your story, something that you do organically when your business is aligned with your mission and values. Kept promises, free returns, follow-up, clean tables and attentive staff are your real marketing. Real marketing creates an impact, leaves a lasting impression and is as powerful as a smile.

THE SECRET TO CREATING IDEAS THAT MATTER

Ability, knowledge, education, money, self-belief and connections all fall away in the face of the one thing that really makes ideas infectious. The success of ideas and dreams of leaders and heroes the world over, from Richard Branson to Steve Jobs, from Scott Harrison (founder of charity:water) to Jacqueline Novogratz (founder and CEO of Acumen Fund), is passion. Passion is the most compelling and irresistible emotion there is.

Passion is at the heart of every idea that matters.

If you want to experience passion selling an idea in action, take a look at how conductor Charles Hazlewood talks about The British ParaOrchestra (www.paraorchestra.com). Charles has founded the world's first world-class orchestra composed entirely of musicians who are disabled. It is a platform for impossible genius, one that can change our perspectives about disability and transform perceptions about what is, and what could be.

If you have this kind of passion, and can communicate your ideas with it, then they will fly.

You can't learn to be passionate, but you can learn how to communicate the passion you already have, by telling the best story you can tell.

DON'T JUST TELL ME
WHAT IT'S MADE OF

Jo is an amazing designer. She creates handmade scarves, from locally woven fabrics which she designs herself. Her website tells part of the story. Jo writes about the materials used and the time it takes to create the design, source just the right fabric dyes and weave the most exquisite scarves you have ever seen. I read all about her passion for her work and why it's important to be unique. I found out that Jo did make beautiful things, but I didn't know why I should care about them.

Until I met her, that is. "You know that you've done the right thing by spending that extra little bit on your scarf, when four or five people in the room stop you to admire it," Jo said. And just like that, I understand why I would want one, not simply because it would look great, but because of how I could imagine myself feeling when I wore it. When Jamie Oliver makes a salad, he talks about the ingredients he's added to make it taste perfect, but he doesn't stop there; he paints a picture of you sharing it with your family and friends.

Don't just make something wonderful; make me a hero.

TALK ABOUT WHAT YOU'RE REALLY SELLING

"In the factories we make perfume, but in the stores we sell hope."
—CHARLES REVLON

What makes clients become regulars and turns customers into evangelists? Most of the time, it isn't what you wrap up for them to take home.

Do you sell photographs or memories? Does your café sell coffee or lifestyle? Does your bookstore sell information or community? Does your pharmacy sell pills or empathy?

At Disney World they don't sell rides; they sell magic. Zappos sells wow, not just shoes. Pandora sells memories, not charms.

Worth emulating?

LOVE IS A MARKETING METRIC

"Put your products, service, website, signage, business cards, every touch point to a simple test. Stand in your customer's shoes and answer one question: what are three things that compel you to say, I love this?"
—KEVIN ROBERTS

Put your energy into creating a product or service that people (maybe not everyone, but enough people) love, and want to buy into.

Here are the only metrics you need:

Did she love it?

Will she come back?

Why?

Why not?

How can we make it better?

REAL ARTISTS DON'T MARKET

Kate is a gifted designer, a true artist. She spends hours foraging through discarded treasures finding just the right fabrics, some that other people would hardly notice. She lovingly puts the fabrics together in her studio, late into the night, and creates one beautiful cushion. This cushion is unique; there isn't another like it in the whole world. It's got history. It's been made by someone who appreciates beauty, who doesn't want to spend her life just working to pay the bills at the end of the week. It contains a tiny piece of Kate's soul. And every day this cushion stays in her online store, not having found a home, a little piece of Kate's soul dies.

"I don't want to do marketing," she protests. "I just want to create my art; artists don't market."

Your art is worthless without a place to call home.

Artists market every day, because they have no choice. They understand that the value of their art is not just in the work and love that went into it, but also in the pleasure it gives once it's got somewhere to live, hands to hold it and people to share it. Artists find ways to tell stories about what they do, with website copy and colour, pictures and blogs.

Artists find ways to make people laugh and cry, believe and covet. Ways to reach into people's hearts and create an emotional connection, with a book, a piece of fabric, a photograph, a design or idea. The best artists market to save their own souls, so they can keep doing the thing that matters.

Marketing is part of your art now.

WHY A BETTER BUSINESS STORY MATTERS

Santoso and Dian live within a kilometre of each other in the once sleepy town of Ubud, in Bali. Both men are master wood-carvers and work for hours every day hunched on the floor of their tiny workshops. Happily for them, Ubud is now the thriving arts centre of the island, and thousands of tourists arrive in buses, cars and taxis every day of the year to shop for souvenirs.

So every day, Santoso and Dian sweep the pavement in front of their workshops and set out row upon row of their amazing hand-carved statues, masks, trinket boxes and trays ready to showcase to their potential customers. The only fly in the ointment is that there are ten equally gifted craftsmen, with similar workshops and shopfronts, all lining up along the same strip, trying to attract same customers. Faced with all that competition, Santoso and Dian can see only one way to differentiate themselves, and that's by being the cheapest woodcarving artisans in the town.

The woodcarvers in Ubud are not much different from the delis on 4th Avenue, the pizza chefs of via San Giovanni or crafters on Etsy. It's all too easy to get stuck in the commodity-and-needs business, when you should really be in the emotional-wants business. What would happen if Dian identified a niche for himself and told his story from a different angle? He might decide to offer woodcarving lessons, with free souvenirs to take home. What if he became not just another woodcarver in Ubud, but *the* woodcarver to go to in Ubud?

> *If we want to be believed and not just noticed, it's time to think about telling a better story.*

So many huge brands—brands like Innocent, Zappos and TED—have built their businesses not on servicing our needs but on appealing to our wants.

How are you selling emotional wants, and not just simple needs, to your clients?

THE BEST IDEAS DON'T START WITH SOLUTIONS

Have you ever wondered why your 'big ideas' get stuck in mind-map central, never to see the light of day, or don't end up being as ground-breaking as you had hoped? Part of the answer lies in the way you've been working on implementing those ideas.

Those moments of genius and excited clarity that you have in the shower tend to start with a beautiful solution. Your ideas often focus on your brilliance and the unique contribution you can make to the world. This is as it should be, but it's not where your planning should start.

Innovation doesn't begin with solutions, it starts at the root of problems.

Don't begin with *your* answers. Start with *their* problems. Be secure in the knowledge that you have the skills and the talent to provide those solutions. There are a million and one Web hosting services on the market. It's hardly a niche. The market is so saturated, why would you consider launching yet another one? That's exactly what Kelly and Ant did with Oz Blog Hosting. Their hosting business doesn't stand out by competing on specs or uptime. They differentiate by understanding the problem that needs to be solved for a tiny niche, and by going narrow and deep.

Kelly realised that the biggest pain point for bloggers was the helplessness they felt when things went wrong. When their site went down, there was nobody local available to answer the phone. Sure, they could get through to a faceless overseas-call-centre operative, but what they really wanted was an unscripted conversation with a real human being. And how many hosting businesses have a picture of the person who answers the phone on their About page?

Kelly and Ant's business provides hosting, but what they actually sell is peace of mind.

They succeed not by being cheaper or more perfect, but by perfectly understanding the problem to solve.

The same opportunity is open to you.

U2 DON'T SING TO EVERYONE

Back in the '80s, when U2 were starting out, they knew they were singing for me and the 520 other girls at my school. It didn't matter that they wrote songs that didn't resonate with my mother. They knew that we drew their album graphics with a Bic Biro on our canvas school bags and scribbled their name on our exercise books during boring history lessons.

Who are you creating for? Who will kill for your designs? Who is going to buy your book or schedule a consultation? Who will understand your message? Hand on heart, do you really know?

It's so easy to overlook this question when you're building your business and crafting your brand.

The creation part—building the thing, scoping out the specs and writing the sales page—is hard enough. So with blind faith we sometimes believe that because we perceive a need and work on fulfilling it, if we build it they will come. Maybe they will, but the thing is, if you create something with a specific audience in mind, then even laying the foundations of your idea becomes so much easier.

Start by knowing your audience;
then build the idea just for them.

Call it what you will: target audience, niche market or client avatar. The label is irrelevant; the purpose is to understand the human being(s) behind that label. That understanding of your audience turns needs into wants and means that you no longer have to use the megaphone to reach people. They will begin to hear you from whispering distance.

One of the best target-audience descriptions I've ever read was written by John Locke. He's the author of the Donavan Creed series of books, among others, and the guy who sold over a million ebooks in five months, so I guess knowing who he's talking to hasn't worked so badly for him. Here's some of what he wrote:

> *The people who love my books love everyday heroes. They are compassionate people who root for the underdog, but are drawn to the outrageous, and have a dry sense of humour. They are all ages, but a surprising number are professional men and women above the age of 50. More than 70% are women. My readers are much more intelligent than you might think, many are doctors nurses and business leaders.*
>
> *Those who like my books tend to be busy people who are frazzled and stressed out beyond the point of no return. They've read their share of high-brow books, but these days they mostly read to relax with a fast-paced easy read that makes them laugh out*

loud. My readers are smarter than my heroes and they know it. They like the small bit of research I do. They don't want to be educated but they love to learn one or two unusual facts along the way they can pass on in conversations at dinner.

How would your products be different if you sat down and created a client avatar like this? Often the hardest thing isn't finding the problem to solve, but understanding the people you want to solve that problem for.

TWENTY WAYS TO TELL
A BETTER BRAND STORY

Customers don't buy your results. They buy the story about the difference those results will make.

1. Name and claim a new category.

2. Clearly articulate what you do, without being boring.

3. Give people a great back-story that explains why you exist, and put it on your About page, in your bio and profiles, and in your other marketing materials.

4. Back up the story by doing great work.

5. Concentrate on speaking to customers with a particular worldview.

6. Paint a picture of the world as it is.

7. Then show your audience the world as it could be.

8. Uncover the essence of a problem and tell the story about how you solve that.

9. Appeal to all senses. Stories aren't just written or spoken.

10. Use a variety of media to convey your message; show and tell.

11. Have a singular purpose and make yourself known for that. This doesn't mean getting stuck in a box. Missions can work across products and industries.

12. Consider what one person says to another to recommend your product, service, or project. Make it easy to share.

13. Speak to your customer's heart, not just her head.

14. Optimise your website for visitors who you want to return, not just traffic that's passing through.

15. Tell people how and why you are different.

16. Avoid using jargon. Simple language works, so write as you would speak.

17. Don't smooth away all the rough edges; be human and authentic. Honesty travels farther than perfection.

18. Be consistent. Everyone in your company must understand your mission and the story you want to tell.

19. Give your customers the opportunity to tell the story and feel a part of it, too.

20. Don't try to be the 'next blank'. A flawed original is better than a perfect imitation.

WORKING ON FOREVER

Do you remember Fran, who booked regular sessions and always opened your newsletter updates? Or Jean, who stopped by for a skinny latte on her way to work every day? How about Jo, who religiously shared your blog posts, and Mark, who sent design clients your way? Have you seen or heard much from them lately?

They were probably the kind of customers, followers and evangelists who didn't spend a fortune or sign up for your top-level coaching program. But they and others like them became your bread and butter over time. Maybe you took them for granted when they were there, but you miss them now that they're gone.

While you are busy building your business, it's easy to forget that no customer is forever. And yet forever is what you should be working on.

Forever takes patience, insight and leaving your ego at the door. Forever is being human, walking in your client's shoes and understanding what your clients want before they know it themselves. Forever means failing, apologising and getting it right next time. Forever comes from creating connection and moments of joy in every interaction. Sometimes forever means treating different customers differently.

Forever is remembering that there are five other juice bars on the same street, and 34 million search results for 'life coach' in Google. Forever means working out what you could be doing better.

How are you working on forever?

YOU ARE THE MAP MAKER

If you invest in that expensive viral marketing campaign, will it definitely work? What's the formula for blog posts that will get the greatest number of retweets? Which new product or service will make you the most money? Do you know?

The truth is that nobody knows for sure what's going to work. If they did, the J.K. Rowlings of this world wouldn't get rejected by twelve publishers. There is no cast-iron guarantee, no secret formula. There is no map to your success.

This means that you are the map maker. You are responsible for shaping your journey and creating your own success.

THE POWER OF ONE

When you're a big ideas person, you have lots of things you want to communicate about your business vision and your brand. In your rush to get all the juicy, good stuff crammed into your pitch, you wind up confusing people. Paring your business idea back to its essence is the answer. Easier said than done, right? How on earth do you communicate all of your value clearly and succinctly?

Start by thinking about and framing just one thing. Craft a single mission. Have one goal. Solve one problem. Close one gap. Find one way to make your clients' lives easier. Get really clear on how you do that, and hey presto, you'll find that your customers suddenly 'get it' and can begin to want it.

Every day you witness the 'power of one' in action, being cleverly executed by some of your favourite brands, like these.

'Innocent' wanted to, as their website says, 'make it easy for people to do themselves some good (whilst making it taste nice too).' They wanted people to think of Innocent drinks as their one healthy habit. Innocent succeeded in creating a *lovemark*— a brand that, as described by Kevin Roberts, inspires loyalty beyond reason—and they built a profitable business by delivering on this single mission.

Zappos was founded in 1999 with the goal of becoming the premiere destination for buying shoes online. Zappos embraced this vision and achieved their goal by doing just one thing: "Delivering wow through service."

KeepCup created the first barista-standard reusable cup and made it the number-one choice for sustainable coffee consumption. The brand and product are founded on one simple belief: that reuse is the most significant environmental impact we can make.

Personal brands have been built on a single idea, too. Robert McKee simply teaches people how to write powerful stories. He teaches his four-day Story Seminar to practicing and aspiring screenwriters all over the world. Entrepreneur Chris Guillebeau—author of *The Art of Non-Conformity* and *The $100 Start-up*—built his brand by helping people to live unconventional lives and change the world.

What's your single mission? What one thing can you promise, communicate and deliver on?

THE QUEST FOR PERFECTION MAKES YOU INVISIBLE

When my three boys were little, our baking days were some of my favourite times. You can picture the scene: sticky, half-licked spoons; flour and chocolate chips everywhere. Those baking days taught me a lot about the value of imperfection.

When a three-year-old is making a gingerbread man, he doesn't ever want to just give him two eyes and three buttons down his middle. He wants to add lots of currants and plenty of mismatched decorations. He will tell you that because *his* gingerbread man is 'special', he doesn't just have three buttons, but wears a coat covered in spots. He also has an extra eye to help him see better. A three-year-old understands the need to mark his guy out, in order to recognise him through the oven door.

I can still remember moments when my self-conscious, perfectionist adult wanted to start rearranging the features of said gingerbread men. To make them neater and perfect. Can you feel your fingers itching to do it, too?

Even if you've never baked gingerbread with a three-year-old, you understand this. That's because you chase perfection every day of your life as you craft your personal brand. You do it on your résumé, in your bio, and in any situation where you feel that your credentials are under scrutiny.

What happens when you are afraid to stand out is that you unconsciously make sure you blend in. You become just like every other gingerbread guy and gal in the bakery, with two eyes and three buttons down the middle and no way in the world to set yourself or your brand apart.

Your tiny differences, flaws and imperfections are what make you unique. Don't be afraid to shine a light on them. Begin today by making a list of your quirky gifts and talents. Think about stories from your past, a time when you didn't fit in, or challenges you may have faced because you are different. Start crafting a real story that people can believe in and care about. Build a window, not a wall.

INCREASE THE VALUE OF YOUR PRODUCTS AND SERVICES FOR FREE

I discovered the most beautiful tea last week. A green tea infused with cherry blossom. I experienced it by accident and would have walked past it on the supermarket shelf. The reason I later paid over $10 for a packet of tea has everything to do with my worldview. The tea was a souvenir of my visit to the place where I first experienced it, and the scent brought back memories of my first home, where two huge pink cherry blossom trees grew in the garden.

It's clear that this is a high-quality product, but what's really disappointing is that there is no story on the packaging. There are too few clues about the history, scent, flavour and the way in which I might experience it. If you're selling a premium product, or if you want to differentiate what you do, you must get better at telling your customers the story.

> *"It doesn't matter how good your idea is if nobody knows."*
> -SALLY HOGSHEAD

The startup AHAlife, which sells carefully selected and curated items, grew 600% this past year by selling people the story behind each product. Founder Shauna Mei recognised that there was a gap in the market, that people needed to understand the passion behind the making and origins of the products in order to recognise their true value.

How is selling the story relevant to your business? What if you don't even sell a physical product?

If you want your idea to succeed, then you need to get better at telling people why it should matter to them. If you want people to understand your quality and your difference, then you need to tell them about it. If you sell something that isn't just about utility (that's 99% of consumer goods and services on the planet), then you need to give people more reasons to care about those things and about you.

It is entirely possible to increase the value of your product or service at no extra cost by telling a better story, just as Hiut Denim, Anthropologie and Lululemon do.

You experience great brand storytelling every single day. Now it's time to put it into practice.

YOU DON'T HAVE A MARKETING PROBLEM

There's something you've convinced yourself of that simply isn't true. Like many people I work with, you are working incredibly hard to produce beautiful products and life-changing services that are not getting the attention they deserve, and you can't understand why your message isn't reaching the people it needs to. So you've convinced yourself you've got a marketing problem. It's time to get really clear on this.

You don't have a marketing problem, and it's highly likely that if you're reading this book, you don't have a product problem, either. What you *do* have is a storytelling problem.

If you are marketing a fabulous product, an innovative application or a life-changing coaching program that isn't selling, then your brand story isn't connecting your audience to the idea.

Take Instagram; it's just a photo-sharing app, right? Wrong. Instagram enables anyone (with a smart phone) to make their life and photos look more spectacular than they really are. For free! It allows users to seamlessly create something beautiful, share it in 60 seconds and get instant feedback, love and adoration from their own audience. Instagram founders Kevin and Mike don't tell the story; they give the users a reason to share it with their friends. The story is baked into the interface.

People don't know why they should be interested in your stuff. It's your job to give them a reason.

THE SECRET TO BUILDING IDEAS THAT FLY

Every single successful idea is born from tapping into just one thing. It's the secret to the success of entrepreneurs the world over, from Arianna Huffington to Richard Branson. You know what it is, but sometimes you get so caught up in creating momentum around your idea that you forget to pay attention to the one thing that really matters.

Ideas that fly are born from discovering neglected worldviews, and then creating something to fill the void.

Each business in the Virgin stable (mobile phones, money, airlines and on and on) was built on this foundation. The neglected worldview is the first perfect brick. Think about any successful business, book, movement or cause you care about and ask yourself the question, 'what neglected worldview did it set out to satisfy?' Amazon, for example, gave us instant access to more books than any bookstore could possibly stock. Zappos created the best online shoe store on the planet by making returns painless and 'delivering joy'.

Take a step back and look at the foundations of this thing you're trying to build. What is your first perfect brick? What void are you filling?

HOW NOT TO NAME A STARTUP OR ANYTHING ELSE

Everyone can agree that there's nothing really objectionable about calling your business 'Bargain World'. It's an innocuous name and most people won't hate it. And that's the problem.

If you're going to name your business, non-profit, product or service something that people won't hate, then you're giving yourself an identity that they will never be able to care about, either.

'Bunkum!' I hear you cry; 'what about Apple and Amazon? Aren't they just unobjectionable words, too?' Back in 1976, when Apple was Apple Computer, tech startups and corporations were called IBM and Microsoft. I bet a few people were laughing behind their hands at the idea of branding an incorporated tech company with a stripey apple. When Jeff Bezos named Amazon after one of the biggest rivers in the world in 1994, other bookstores were called Borders Books and Waldenbooks. It didn't take people long to fall in love with Amazon, which of course aspired to be the biggest, fastest, get-what-you-want bookstore (that had room to grow, not to be just a bookstore) in the world.

Your business or product name is the hook on which you hang your story and start the conversation with customers. It's the mechanism you give people to identify you. And when you earn their trust and loyalty, it's the way they spread the news about you. Your brand and product names are some of the most priceless assets your business can own. They should make you stand out, not fit in.

If nobody can find an objection to the brand name you choose, then you've probably got the wrong name. This kind of brand naming architecture often happens by committee, which means that you end up with something that will be forgotten. Your name should polarize people, spark their interest and make them want to get to know more about what you do.

Here's a simple test. If you can't imagine someone wanting to wear your name on a T-shirt one day, then it's probably not the right name for you now.

THE IPHONE DOESN'T MATTER TO EVERYONE

Ideas that matter, spread.

If you want anything you conceive, launch, or care about to succeed, then you've got to make it matter first. I'm not talking about mattering for a day while your offer is on Groupon, or mattering during your opening-week buzz. I mean 'really' mattering. The kind of mattering that makes people cross the road (or town), passing your competitors on the way, to buy from you. The sort of mattering that touches people in a place way deeper than their pockets.

This might be the cue to throw your hands in the air and give up, because you wonder how your thing can ever matter *that* much. But wait… I haven't gotten to the best bit.

You don't need to matter to everyone.

In fact, you positively don't want to matter to the whole universe. Quite the opposite. You can succeed by simply mattering more to the few.

Apple has 5% of the global mobile-phone market share. They're doing okay mattering just to the few. Make your market tiny.

Create significance for the people on the sidelines. Investigate the edges. Quit trying to please everyone, and instead, woo a handful.

Whisper softly to the people who want to hear from you. Then you'll matter.

YOUR BEST IDEA MIGHT BE THE ONE PEOPLE LAUGH AT

Imagine a quiet dinner early in 1984, where over a few drinks, Richard Branson announces his plans to a few close friends. He explains that he is going to cream some of the profits from his successful Virgin Records business and use it to lease a second-hand Boeing 747. His intention is to start a commercial airline and take on the mighty British Airways in the process.

Some people would have thought it was a joke and actually laughed aloud. Others, their forks suspended in mid-air, might have looked him dead in the eye to work out if he really was joking or if he had finally gone mad.

How many times in his business career do you think that Richard Branson was laughed at? Considering that he went from being the dyslexic teen editor of a magazine to having a vision of galactic missions and changing the face of every industry from money to health care, I'm guessing quite a few.

People will probably laugh at you, too.

They will laugh at your ideas, both big and small. Those devil's advocates will challenge your vision of the world as it could be. They will tell you it can't be done. Just like they told Muhammad Yunus, founder of the Grameen Bank in Bangladesh, that the poor wouldn't pay back their micro-loans. The naysayers will urge you to be careful.

People will call on you to be realistic and sensible. Just like them. They will urge you to wait for the 'right time'. And maybe you will.

You might wait to work on the idea that simply can't fail. Why? Because you don't want to feel like you are six years old again. Because you can't bear the thought of putting something imperfect out into the world. Something that might fail.

That would-be failure you're working on, like Virgin Atlantic Airways, will never become something that has a chance to succeed unless you get over the fear of having ideas that people will laugh at, and you begin having enough faith in your ideas (and yourself) to put them to work.

YOUR CUSTOMER IS THE HERO

I know your products are beautiful. I also read on the packaging that your juice is packed full of vitamins. And anyone with an eye can see that your designs are amazing.

But knowing all the facts about how great you are and how well made your stuff is will never be what makes your customers reach for their wallets.

The only way to persuade people to care about you is to show that you care about them first. Make them the hero of your story. This doesn't mean starting again from scratch or making up a pile of stuff about your brand or business. You've already got the product, the great cause, the proof and the results. Now all you need to do is tell the story from a different angle. Just as {r}evolution apparel did when they launched a sustainable fashion brand for the restless. For customers who cared about where their clothes came from, {r}evolution apparel told them about conscious consumption. They showed customers that they didn't need more stuff to be happy. And their idea took off.

DIFFERENT ENOUGH

Most restaurants tell a similar story (or try to, anyway): 'We serve the best food.' Every non-profit tells us how our money will make an impact, and every box of detergent promises to clean clothes better than the pack next to it.

So how are you going to tell a different story? One that's not for everyone.

What other promises can you make and keep? What priceless shortcuts can you offer? What will enable people to connect with your brand? What will make them choose you?

Could you tell a story as different as Sanuk's, the footwear brand selling shoes, designed with 'barefoot untechnology', that are so comfortable, they don't feel like shoes at all?

How are you going to tell a story that's different enough to get noticed, and true enough to be believed? And who are you going to tell it to?

THEY'RE TELLING YOUR STORY

You work hard to create an impression of your brand or business. To make your idea spread. You tell the story with your packaging, website design, logo, products, copy and service. You share it in print, in video, at events and on online networks. Those impressions you work to create are only a tiny part of what makes up the complete picture of your brand.

Of 146 million views generated for Coca-Cola on YouTube, 26 million were generated by Coke, and 120 million views were generated by consumers!

> *"Who's controlling the dialogue? It's not me."*
> —WENDY CLARK, VP MARKETING, COCA-COLA

Now your business has a fantastic opportunity to engage with customers and fans, to enter into a dialogue, to listen, to reach out to them and understand how and why they use, love or hate your product.

You might have the trademark, you might even wear the crown, but you don't own the story.

What you do have, though, is an opportunity like never before to give your customers a great story to tell.

HOW TO SPREAD AN IDEA

*"Everyone who's ever taken a shower has an idea.
It's the person who gets out of the shower, dries off
and does something about it who makes a difference."*
—NOLAN BUSHNELL

So how do you begin to make an impact and spread an idea?

1. Create something that people want to talk about.

2. Give people a way to share it.

3. Know who you are talking to or targeting.

4. Understand your audience.

5. Work out what people want before they do.

6. Think about what one person will say to another to recommend it.

7. Question why someone will buy, use, or talk about your product or service over another.

8. Believe in the idea yourself.

9. Be the best choice.

10. Create for a few.

11. Make it work for the many.

12. Ask people to try it.

13. Engage people and build trust.

14. Connect your true fans.

15. Help people to care about what you do or sell.

16. Ask your followers to share it.

17. Make people laugh.

18. Make people cry.

19. Do something unexpected.

20. Be generous.

21. Promise something and deliver on it.

22. Create something people want, not just something they need.

23.   Be passionate.

24.   Start!

25.   Evaluate and make it better.

FRAMING YOUR SCARCITY

Don't be shy about telling the real story of what you make or do. Point out how your designs brought a brand to life. How your coaching helped someone to do the thing they'd always wanted to do. Tell people the story of how your work changed how people feel. Show them how you take people from where they are to where they want to be.

Understanding and acknowledging (often to yourself) what's rare or unique about what you do, or how and why you do it, is the key.

Perhaps you make beautiful one-off silk scarves? Maybe you work with only two design clients at a time? Do you have the ability to stop people from censoring their dreams? Or maybe you're launching an event that sells to just 140 people? Have you spent the best part of four years bringing about the dream of opening an artisan bakery, like The Orange Boot, that opens for only six hours and sells out of a tiny selection of freshly baked bread every day?

Unless you're making brass thumbtacks, there is an element of scarcity in what you do and how and why you do it, a combination of your story and your superpower.

Find the right words to communicate that. Set yourself apart.

Then hold your head high and double your prices.

SIX QUESTIONS FOR CRAFTING YOUR BRAND RELEVANCE

1. Who do we want to care about what we sell or do?

2. Why would those people care about what we do or what we are selling?

3. Why would they cross the street to buy from us?

4. What emotional want are we fulfilling?

5. How can we make this more about them and less about us?

6. What will they be able to say to their friends to recommend us?

We need to give people one reason to care about us, not just a hundred different reasons to buy from us.

WHY MAGICAL BEATS LOGICAL

If customers bought everything based purely on logic, then Jimmy Choo would be out of business and everyone would be buying shoes from Target.

If every product sold purely because of its features and benefits alone, then Alex wouldn't be willing to wait (first in line) overnight outside the Apple store in Sydney so he could be one of the first to own an iPad 2 the next morning. When I asked him (through the magic of Twitter) why he would do that, he told me it was 90% passion, people, and excitement and 10% product. He's there for the story he can tell himself, for the "excitement of meeting people from all over with a common passion for something, a goal."

Your customers want you to tell them these kinds of stories, too. They want to get excited about what you do. They want to trust you to keep your promises. They want to connect and belong, to share in the story.

Most of all, they want your brand and your products to be unique, incredible and magical so that they can feel that way, too.

THE INTERNET IS NOT A SHORTCUT

Here is the cold hard truth about the Internet, viral marketing and the way to make your ideas matter.

The Internet gives you a million and one chances to amplify what's great about what you do. It doesn't actually make your idea better.

A hundred thousand people found Philippa Stanton on Instagram. But she was an amazing visual storyteller, a synesthetic artist whose work touched people, long before she downloaded the Instagram app.

There's only one formula for getting your work noticed over and over again.

Do good work.

Then do it over and over again.

If you do good work, people will find you. If you give them something to come back for, they'll keep coming back. And if you make them care, they'll share you with their friends.

THE DIFFERENCE BETWEEN TRAFFIC AND VISITORS

When you optimise your website for 'traffic', are you doing your best work?

Working out how to get 'traffic' to find you is a tactic, which anyone can win at if they have technical support. Giving 'visitors' a reason to stay, though, means having a strategy for creating great content that can't be easily duplicated.

'Traffic' is passing through. Far better to think in terms of how you can turn a visitor into someone who cares to return.

Tiny distinctions make all the difference.

ARE YOU MEASURING WHAT MATTERS?

The bistro owner thinks that what's most important is getting customers seated and served quickly. Because she believes that her customers simply value tidy lines and orders pushed through, she creates standards and key performance indicators. She measures things that enable her staff to tick boxes and make them look hunted.

The truth is, people don't visit her bistro in order to tell themselves a story about how they got fed quickly, for three times the cost of making a salad at home. When they want quick, there's always McDonald's.

Your metrics should be created around what's most important to your customer. Is he looking for a shortcut, reassurance or love? Whatever it is, you need to understand it and deliver it in spades.

Businesses and brands succeed when they deliver value based on customers' wants, not on the metrics of a well-oiled machine.

ATTENTION IS NOT THE PROBLEM

You might have access to a hundred and one new channels that allow you to broadcast a message, but there are only a handful of ways to get attention for your idea.

1. Advertising
The old and expensive way to buy attention. You might be able to buy eyeballs, but you can't guarantee that you're changing minds.

2. Sales
You can beg people for attention by using a sales team or social media. But people become tired of dealing with interruptions they don't want.

3. Public relations
You could join the public relations lottery and keep waiting for the call from Oprah. It's a long shot.

4. Earning it
Alternatively, you could just focus on solving people's problems and creating something people value.

Build what you're building for engagement, not just attention. Beloved brands, favourite restaurants, and cherished products are always built to be loved.

Attention in isolation is overrated, and it's not what makes ideas that matter.

BEING THE MOST

In the '80s, Starbucks set out to be the most inspiring coffee brand on the planet. When they forgot this in the '90s and tried becoming the most ubiquitous, they lost their way.

If you could be 'the most' to people, what 'most' would you be?

Most reliable.
Most irresistible.
Most ubiquitous.
Most loved.
Most ——————.

You get to choose.

WHAT DOES
THE COMPETITION DO?

I was consulting with two financial planners this week. We were discussing what made them different, when they told me this story about working with one of their clients.

Jonathan was offered $9 million for his house, which had amazing, never-to-be-replaced views out over the river. He was in a quandary about what to do. Most advisers (thinking about maximising the return of a portfolio) would have told him to make hay, sell immediately, take the equity and reinvest it.

Not Mark. He sat out on the balcony with Jonathan and chatted to him about his personal and life goals. They talked about why Jonathan had chosen to live there in the first place. Mark encouraged him to imagine what life would be like with the money in the bank, but no view. Jonathan decided to walk away from the $9 million, which could never replace the feeling he got every day by just living comfortably where he was.

No surprise then that Mark and his partner don't need to advertise, and that 95% of their business is generated by word of mouth.

Work out how you are *least* like the competition, then tell that story.

BECAUSE IT MATTERS

How do you stand out when there are two other juice bars on the same street, and half a dozen 'good-enough' life coaches just three clicks away?

If you've got the same choices as the competition, how you choose can make all the difference.

Do you make decisions based on what's gone before, or do you change everything?

Are you doing what you do because if feels safe, or because it matters?

Same amount of effort, big difference.

THE SURE THING

If you've ever watched surfers, you'll know that they spend far more time reading the waves than riding them. And despite all of the waiting, watching and experience, they still sometimes choose the wrong wave to ride. In the end they take their best guess, commit and go.

And so it goes for ideas, too.

Did Pinterest co-founder Ben Silbermann know, back in 2009, that he was building what would become the fastest growing social network? And did Kevin Systrom have any idea that his Instagram app would be acquired by Facebook for a billion, just months after the film and camera company Kodak went bankrupt?

Nobody knows for sure. There is no certainty. No such thing as a 'sure thing'.

So once you've done the preparation, there is no reason not to take your best guess and go.

The people who succeed are the ones who put the need for certainty aside, to focus on riding the best wave they can. They don't wait for the tide to be perfect tomorrow.

ACKNOWLEDGMENTS

Without readers, there would be no writers.
Thank you to my blog readers (and you), who make me care about showing up every day.

Without heroes, there would be no reminders not to sell ourselves short.
Thanks to Seth Godin, for teaching me everything I know about showing up and making art, and for helping me to understand that the goal is to get to play again tomorrow.

Without editors, there would be no clarity.
Thanks to Catherine Oliver, for making sense of my thoughts and words.

Without designers, there would be no beautiful way to interpret the world.
Thanks to Reese Spykerman, for designing truths and caring so much about making ideas matter.

Without love, there would be no reason to keep going.
Thank you above all, to Moyez, Adam, Kieran and Matthew, who are the reason that I do.

Made in the USA
Lexington, KY
08 December 2012